BORDER

1921-2021 – A Centennial Calibration

DARACH MacDONALD

Colmcille
Press

In loving memory of
Mamo
1929-2021
poet, feminist, activist, confidante,
inspirational speaker and my mother.

Published December 2021
COLMCILLE PRESS
Ráth Mór Centre
Bligh's Lane, Derry BT48 0LZ
www.colmcillepress.com

Front cover image: Rita Duffy, Segregation, 1989. Collection Crawford Art Gallery, Cork.
© The artist.

Edited by Garbhán Downey
Layout/design by Joe McAllister, Hive Studios – www.hivestudio.org

ISBN 978 1 914009 26 6
A CIP catalogue record for this book is available from the British Library.

ACKNOWLEDGEMENTS

Few images capture so vividly the trauma of enforced separation as Rita Duffy's 1989 painting 'Segregation', used on the cover of this book. I gratefully acknowledge the kind permission of the artist to use this image and the assistance of Dr Michael Waldron, assistant curator of the Crawford Gallery of Cork, where the painting now resides.

I would also like to thank Frank Rafferty, director of the Bluebell Arts Centre in Derry, for several opportunities to test run segments of Border 1921-2021at Poetry Trail readings and at an event filmed by John O'Neill in an online work entitled Village Poets. In a period of pandemic lockdown, the peer review feedback from these events was invaluable.

I am hugely grateful to Colmcille Press and its publisher Garbhan Downey for taking this on board from the outset and for ensuring that the centennial year of the border would not pass without this poetic calibration.

I also wish to acknowledge the support of the Arts Council for Northern Ireland/National Lottery through the Support for the Individual Artist Programme (SIAP) in the completion of this work.

The John Bryson
Foundation

ABOUT THE AUTHOR

Darach MacDonald is a journalist and author who has been writing professionally about the border for almost half a century.

Born and raised in Clones, County Monaghan, he studied at University College Dublin where his 1976 MA thesis in History was on the 'wishes of the inhabitants' as outlined in submissions to the Irish Boundary Commission 1924-25.

As a journalist with Hibernia National Review, Independent Newspapers, the *Sunday Tribune* and the Irish Press Group, he wrote extensively about the political and economic impact of the Troubles on border communities.

Having lived and worked in Canada for ten years (1987-1997) he returned to Ireland and completed his 1998 novel, *The Sons of Levi*, telling the story of Ulster Protestant loyalists from Monaghan who were consigned to the Irish Free State when excluded from the new Northern Ireland.

While writing for various newspapers in Ireland, Britain, Canada and the United States, he completed his 2000 non-fiction book, *The Chosen Fews: Exploding Myths in South Armagh*. This described the impact of partition on an overwhelmingly nationalist community that had been recommended for transfer to the Free State in the shelved Boundary Commission report.

On retiring as editor of the Omagh-based Ulster Herald newspaper group, Darach moved to a loyalist housing estate in Castlederg to write *Blood & Thunder: Inside a Protestant Marching Band* (2010). He remained there for five years researching his 2015 doctoral thesis, Proud to be Prod: Music, Memory and Motivation in an Ulster loyalist band (Ulster University, Magee).

That ethnographic study of a frontier loyalist community centred on the Castlederg Young Loyalists flute band that has been 'marching along the border' since its formation in the mid-1970s.

Dr Darach MacDonald drew on his family background, his lived experiences, his education and academic research, as well as his journalistic expertise, to write *Hard Border: Walking through a Century of Irish Partition* (2018), a sweeping pre-Brexit insight into border communities along the route of the disused Ulster Canal that once connected Lough Erne to Lough Neagh, encompassing five of Ulster's nine counties – Cavan, Fermanagh, Monaghan, Armagh and Tyrone.

He now lives in the border city of Derry where he continues to write and deliver talks on matters relating to partition and the border, between cross-border forays for walks on Donegal's hills and beaches.

Other books by Darach MacDonald

The Sons of Levi (1998)

The Chosen Fews: Exploding Myths in South Armagh (2000)

Blood & Thunder: Inside an Ulster Protestant Band (2010)

Tochar: Walking Ireland's Ancient Pilgrim Paths (2014)

Hard Border: Walking through a Century of Irish Partition (2018)

Ireland's Pilgrim Paths: Walking the Ancient Trails (2020)

FOREWORD by Eoin Mcnamee

Start with the line itself. It's Victor Orban's razor wire. It's Donald Trump's border wall. It crumbles into the sand but appears elsewhere. The Berlin Wall becomes peace lines in Belfast, becomes walled-off settler roads and enclosures in the West Bank.

A border is the outworking of the authoritarian imagination. It looks backwards and forwards, hoards its history, plots its future.

We see borders as consequences of political forces but they are in fact an end in themselves. The currency of the frontier is spent bullet casings, binbagged corpses, riddled gospel halls.

The border genre is dystopia, society in dissolution, everything broken down. Militias emerge from the darkness and return to it. Everyone is watching everyone else and you can't get a grip on any of it. You're asking yourself how did we come to this, who brought us here?

Lately I was sitting in a quiet house on Bóthar na Sop in Ballina, the straw road laid for Napoleon's soldiers to march inland from Killala in 1798. I was with a Chinese friend whose grandfather was a Kuomintang general, forced to flee and abandon his new wife. The Chinese Revolution and Napoleon's imperial ambitions meet in that quiet house.

It is a mistake to characterise our quiet places as peripheral. Our border is central to Europe and therefore to the world and the slaughter of world war echoes through it as it is being used to prise open the European Union. The danger is not that the border is a physical thing, the peril lies in its abstractions.

It is not simply that borders divide but that they exist outside the rules, beyond moral authority and therefore open to the most malign of uses.

Darach MacDonald captures the personal, political and historical overtones but he's also alive to the hallucinatory force of it, the malign future taking place in front of our eyes, and under our feet.

Eoin McNamee

PROLOGUE

We were bemused when it first appeared
That brand new border line that seared
Three hundred miles long, not half an inch thick
It would surely be gone in no more than a tick.

For that line was never meant to be
More than a temporary boundary.
We trusted Feetham, Fisher and MacNeill[1]
To make huge transfers, not a backroom deal.

Fermanagh, Tyrone and Derry City left out
South Armagh and the Mournes moved to the south.
What would be left up north could never persist
And the border would vanish into our Celtic mist.

But a century later, it still stands square
Except up close where it's not even there
An imaginary line that cuts to our bones,
Further back you go, the more real it becomes.

Still it lingers in the mind long after,
Framing those years of strife and slaughter,
A man-made feature of geography
Even Google now follows its trajectory.

Yet this line that circumscribes our lives
Exists in many forms and guises
Changing often it befuddles and deceives
And its districts come in all shapes and sizes.

CEANNTAR I

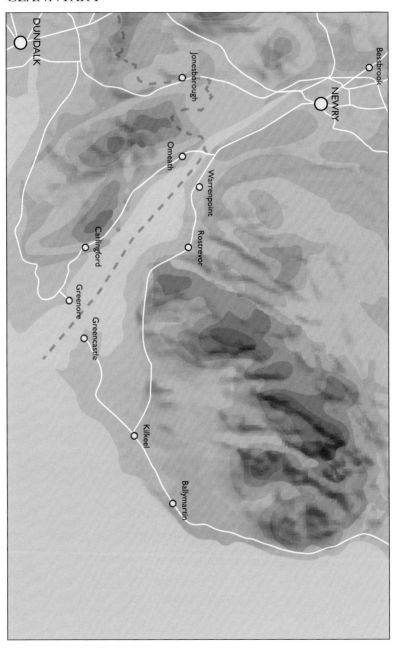

CEANNTAR I

For centuries they've glared at each other
Twin sentinels at the mouth of a border:
Greenore and its Lordship long shorn
From Greencastle's Kingdom of Mourne.

Muirhevna's Plain and Cooley country
Were part of Ulster once, you see
But now from Kilkeel to Ardee
Louth voices fall Down to a Silent Valley.

In times past, Mac Aonghusa looked down
From Slievefadda, Slieveban and Knockshee
To see the advance of England's Crown
On Foye, Eagle's Rock and Anglesey.

Then as the waters widen and narrow back
Each stronghold matched across the lough
Carlingford, Rostrevor, Warrenpoint, Omeath
Meeting where Newry pulls away from Dundalk.

When a Royal Mint and King John's Keep [2]
Once marked a Pale that England could reap
Stout Bagenal's Castle was a means to prevail
In the war to bridle the Cineal Uí Néill. [3]

Yet a rebellious spirit survived in Newry
Nurtured by Mitchel, de Valera and Rowntree[4]
Until the roadside slaughter of a Miami showband[5]
Where civil rights marchers had made their stand.

When the North erupted, families broke for the border
Many stayed on and that caused some disorder
In a town dubbed El Paso that remained on the brink
With a Heavy Gang[6] and subversion fuelled by drink.

The border was a battlefield from the very get go
And among those it claimed were Oliver[7] and Ludlow[8],
Until the RUC top brass drove home by Edenappa
And Buchanan and Breen were slain in the trap.[9]

Then modern warriors at Narrow Water Keep
Gathered charred flesh as they waded knee deep
Picking up fragments of their young comrades lost
When blown to kingdom come in an IRA double blast.[10]

And where a hotel once stood, police still count the cost
In a score of their officers whose lives were lost;
Nearly half of them died in a single onslaught
As mortars rained down and flattened their fort.[11]

Then the fog descends on a Parisian wood
Where my old friend Ruddy, his head in a hood, [12]
Was tortured and killed as if to presage
His hometown consumed by that Killing Rage.[13]

Until a peace train shunted across Craigmore
Sweeping away much that went on before
And new prosperity beckoned for shopping
As 'N–euro' reversed the old border-hopping.

Rising up from the Marshes, a new city charter
Shrugs off its troubles as southerners barter
While on mobile phones they loudly chatter
And stare wide-eyed at the price of life's water.

Back in the south a wounded Tiger licks a sore
And stretches its limbs to roar out once more
In a lair of pristine malls ringed by a fence
Of new highways and 'Corr blimey' confidence.[14]

Now where twin customs and army scrutineers
Once kept up their constant reconnoitres
A motorway sweeps along by Edentubber
With not even a nod to the rebel martyrs.[15]

For this has always been frontier terrain,
The ancient playground of Cúchulainn
Each faltering foothold fought for and won
Beneath the brow of Flagstaff's frown.

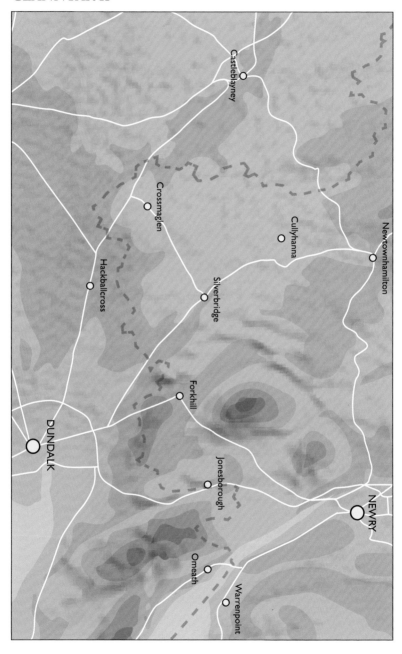

CEANNTAR II

By the Gap o' the North and the Three Steps Bar
We enter the Ring of Gullion and South Armagh
A place once avoided because of cloak and dagger,
Its people had to endure that military swagger.

Where O'Hanlon once ruled over his terrain
Slieve Gullion still presents its rich domain
And Croslieve presides over Mullaghbawn's plain
As squaddies look down with hilltop disdain

On a fabled land of night cattle drives across
Forkhill's roads into Inniskeen, Hackballscross
And Faughart where pilgrims still come to pray
At the sacred shrine of Naomh Bríd of the Gael.

This holy place desecrated and shocked
Also sweeps north by a crooked lough
To Aiken's home and back by the courses[16]
Of a train of slaughter for all the King's horses.[17]

Then west to Cross' over a Silverbridge
Of Creggan, Sheelagh and Cullyhanna's ridge,
Where Mac Lionnáin nestled in their charms
Until ringed by towers and men at arms.

It's hard now to believe this quiet wee spot
Changed so completely when Harry was shot.[18]
Then Provo recruits rallied to McVerry's call
And soon became the very deadliest of them all.[19]

But with cock assurance 'Danny Boy' set out[20]
To tame and cajole this defiant redoubt
And by night he played at his own dirty game
Shifting between sides to stack up the blame

For a bloody sequence of deadly tit-for-tat
Flowing from the Miami massacre so that
Tullyvallen, Donnelly's, the Reavys, Kingsmills
Were added to a catalogue of mindless kills.[21]

Peter Cleary taken out in the dead of night [22]
Wee Majella shot by day through a soldier's sight[23]
Troopers Benner, Borucki and so many more[24]
It soon defied efforts to keep track of the score.

SAS on the ground and choppers in the air
This once quiet place soon caught in the glare
Of the media that never stopped to ask why
It was outlawed and reviled as 'Bandit Country'.

And as the watchtowers rose above this place
Those hostile outsiders deemed it a disgrace
That forces of the Crown were not free to roam
Though a part of Ireland that was never their home.

For in Creggan churchyard lie poets of a nation
Who kept alive their rich Gaelic civilisation
Long after the Fews had failed to convince
Until recalled with pride by a scholarly prince.[25]

For this is a land of Pavee winks and nodding
Except at Brit soldiers 'not even worth ignoring',[26]
A place of learning and furtive glances
Across the floor, too, at 'Blayney dances.

All this was destined for the Free State
Until that backroom deal sealed its sad fate[27]
Consigning it once more to Britannia's rule
And the 'Bandit Country' tag of a political fool.[28]

From Bessbrook Mill, a tangled web they spin[29]
Over these far-flung frontiers of HM's reign
Until their hill-top posts were toppled flat
They left at last and 'go Nairac an bóthar leat'.

CEANNTAR III

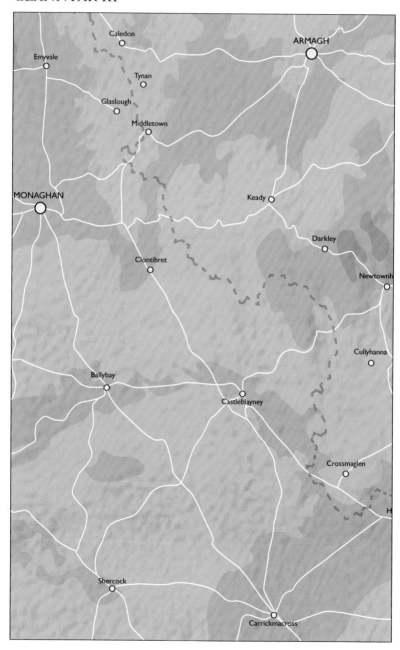

CEANNTAR III

From Blayney's Castle we now head north
Through the 'Scotch country' districts that start[30]
At Mullyash lodges once hoping to switch
To the other side of a new Dorsey ditch.[31]

Through Hamilton's new town that sits on the fringe
Of Darkley times where murder and mayhem impinge
On lonely gospel halls[32], while a death squad cringes,
In UDR uniforms for more victims to extinguish.[33]

Yet tucked together like foetal twins on the map
These Oriel counties continued to trade and swap.[34]
But don't bother asking as they move along sprightly
On unapproved roads, 'Och sure, they'll do us rightly!'

Past Keady town and wild Derrynoose
A Fergort Road twists like the neck of a goose
To Clontibret where O'Neill once vanquished,[35]
Robin's son came to boast and then was banished.[36]

Past the ruined remains of once stout Castleshane
We swing west to inspect and perhaps even detain
Where Monaghan town presides in all of its glory
Staunchly Protestant once, but that's another story. [37]

Honouring an officer of the Crown with stately aplomb
A huge obelisk in Church Square still looks down[38]
From its lofty vantage over a county town
Where seven lives were ripped apart in a UVF bomb.[39]

Yet through the decades of trouble and strife
They flocked here from the North to experience life
Not fixed from birth by who or what you are
They saw it distorted through glass in a bar.

For lurking right here and plotting away
Were squads of volunteers of the Provo IRA
With Lynagh and others yet destined to fall
On a night when the SAS lay in wait at Loughgall.[40]

Back to that line, we move off once again
By Silverstream roads where once Hand and Pen[41]
Orangemen marched along to a different tune
And so we now bear down on Middletown.

Another huge fortress here blocked the way
From Eamon Donnelly's[42] home to Armagh City
Where repose the remains of King Brian Boru
A holy double See, but a troubled way through.

Here city status sits uneasily on a town's
Picturesque Mall and stately homes
Where Ussher once charted his outlay
Of where we began until our Judgement Day.[43]

Yet where Patrick brought Macha hope of salvation
Her children staked out rival views of the nation
The Orange and Green pitted in a deadly battle
With gunfire, bombs and a deafening drum rattle.

From the Diamond affray the rival sides began
To roll back Enlightenment and the Rights of Man,
Dividing the United Irishmen into 'them' and 'us'
And obliterating Henry Joy in the loyalist cause.[44]

The gap was taken up by a gang from Glenanne[45]
Whose bloodletting started and then ran and ran
And into the mix rode a deadly Border Fox[46]
Whose tour of terror defied all border roadblocks.

So down the years since that point in time,
Armagh has been tainted with sectarian grime.
It's a holy demise but what a dreadful pity
For a place once vaunted as our agreed capital city.[47]

CEANNTAR IV

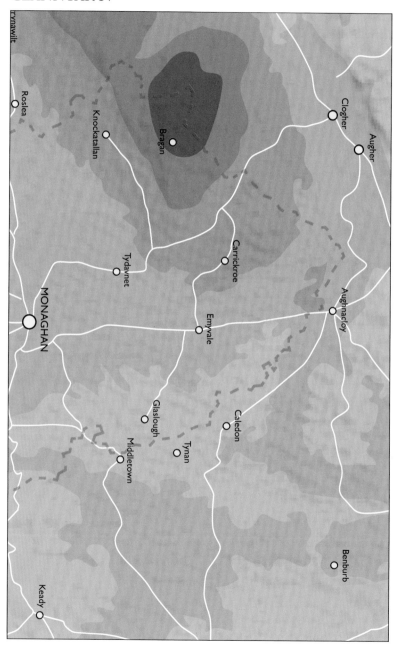

CEANNTAR IV

Back on our fickle frontier, meanwhile
Three Ulster counties converge at a stile
Linking Glaslough with Tynan and Caledon
Leslies, Alexanders and the family Stronge.

Sprung from one stock but of varied allegiance
Neighbours living on the frontiers of tolerance
Until the Stronges were butchered in the dead of night
And historic Tynan Abbey was then set alight.[48]

Recoiling from such horror, we first make our way
Where Rising Sons of William thunder through Killylea
Then into Tyrone where civil rights calls began
When an MP's girl's house couldn't go to her B man.[49]

Back in the day, fierce gun battles raged here
With squadrons of Specials sent to ward off the fear
While upstart rebels who now had their Free State
Rattled with British guns to get through the gate.[50]

Craigavon was the rock, and he stood his ground
To hold Clogher's Valley and all the way round.[51]
But just beyond Moybridge we pause where we should
For young Aidan McAnespie shot down in cold blood.[52]

For the IRA this district's a cradle for heroes
From the first blanket man to die in the throes,
McCaughey, Hartes, McKearneys and many others
Their roll of honour is a list of lost brothers.[53]

Yet for those on the other side of the fence
There's always a uniform to don for defence
A, B and C Specials, RUC and UDR
An alphabet of security to notch up the score.

The east Tyrone IRA sowed Protestant fear here
When they slaughtered eight squaddies and four UDR,[54]
But the Glenanne UVF had brought a fresh angle
By adding this district to its murder triangle.

Now here on the main Dublin to Derry highway
An ominous checkpoint has now given way
To a road sign that makes intercity traffic wait
As a tractor trundles by and heads for a gate.

So further into the Valley we make our way out
Shunning Ballygawley and its double roundabout
From our true quest now we cannot waver
As we set off in search of a Royal Favour.

But a stately ruin is all that is left to tell
Of that long-ago night when they seized Ankatell
Dragging him off by their own cruel whims
As the old man sang out loudly his loyalist hymns.[55]

Through every phase of strife and trouble
This was an armed bastion, a loyalist bubble.
South of Blackwater, but still in the North
A republican bought it, for what that is worth.

In a high mountain bog at a wild place called Bragan
Great diggers are poking the sod and dragging
In hopes of finding poor Columba's remains
Shot in the head in '75 and just dumped in its drains.[56]

Monaghan sticks up into County Tyrone here
A sharp trajectory British generals dubbed the 'Spur'
Where McKennas meet O'Neills and all the way up
They cheered as Canavan carried home Maguire's cup.[57]

Past Augher to Clogher's village Cathedral city
Where Macartan of Oriel rooted his Christianity
But bitter words, fear and threats still divide
Christians from those who are on the other side.

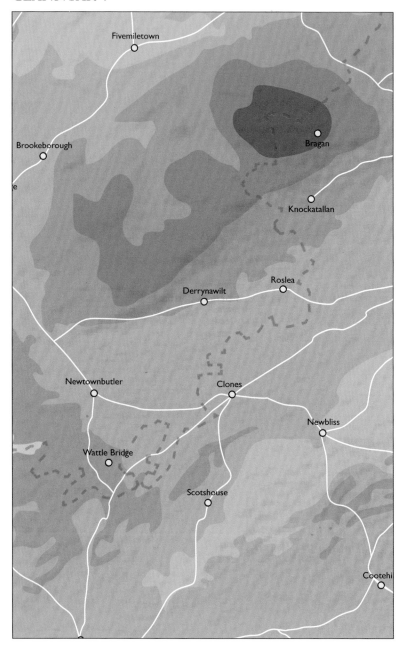

CEANNTAR V

In a high lake hollow where three counties meet
Near Sean Bearna's Stables they gather to greet
Neighbours from Tydavnet, Clogher and Roslea.
Three counties, three parishes converged on Slieve Beagh. [58]

Up where the rapparee once hunted and harried
The young volunteer McElwain never tarried
Until gunned down by the SAS in a border trap
And shot dead in the head to halt his gallop. [59]

In his native Knockatallan he still makes his mark
In a memorial to match another at nearby Altawark
Where South and O'Hanlon are recalled to tell
For generations of rebels this has been a crucible. [60]

The border has been erupting here since back in the day
When Spencer was shot, and the Specials burnt Roslea [61]
The IRA came out in force and they shot three more
And the daggers were drawn as both sides went to war.

So around Dernawilt Cross in the foothills below,
Loyalists don uniforms and take up arms to show
That might is still right and always on their side
Yet when they're killed it's called religious genocide.

Past Inver and Lackey into Clones town we now go
By a Blind Lough where Stewart defeated Owen Roe[62]
It was perched on the cusp of a new Free State
Cheek-by-jowl with the line that would seal its sad fate.

At the foot of the town in the old railway station
A pivotal act marked the split of a divided nation
Four Specials and Fitzpatrick were killed in the affray
Causing both sides to dig in and go their own way.[63]

This was once the hub of the old GNR
A pivotal rail junction for all of south Ulster
Partition, of course, changed all of that
Within a few decades the town was busted flat.

It's another district where the roads are jumbled
Impossible to tell whenever you've stumbled
From north to south and then turn about,
'Til the Brits blasted craters to remove any doubt.[64]

At first people came to protest and toil
At opening those roads while hoping to foil
The might of an empire digging its last ditch
To seal its terrain from any thoughts of a switch.

Then Creighton, Bell, young Murray and Naan[65]
The death list began, and it just ran and ran
Until a 'mongrel' Fox was finally run to ground
Bleeding to death in a ditch with barely a sound.[66]

A tidal shift followed from that dreadful day
As the Dublin government turned sharply away
From a town marooned, a parish split
Then slowly starved of life, a treble hit.

Shoved to the side and so readily forgotten,
A community in crisis and its misbegotten
Sons sent to jail for what they still held as true;
Acts of patriotism to them, just terrorism to you.[67]

Yet even in the darkness as all hope disappeared
A young boxer emerged and all Ulster cheered
When he brought home a world featherweight Crown,
'Leave the fighting to McGuigan' and save his home town.[68]

But jobs lost and moved, while shops shut their doors
The town withered and died from its festering sores.
Yet year after year for Ulster finals of the GAA
It rolled out its frayed carpet to put on a display.

By Drumully's lost townlands we now take our leave
Encircled by the border, cut off from reprieve[69]
Along an abandoned canal we'll take our last hike,
Where a Black Pig once guarded its own Ulster dyke.

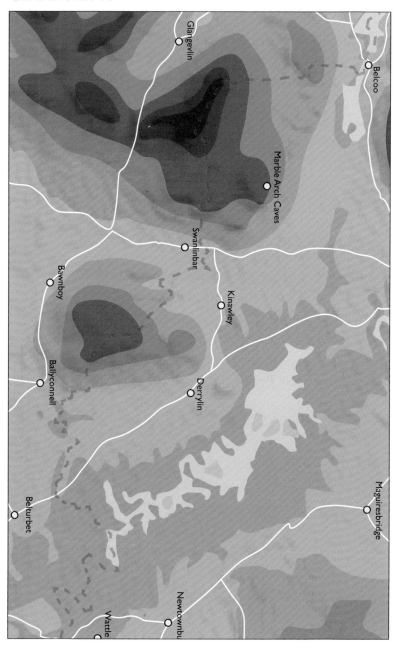

CEANNTAR VI

Past Wattlebridge where old songs of Erne
Tell of Williamite slaughter, we now take a turn[70]
To the west where the border sweeps on
By once sturdy, now gutted Castle Saunderson.[71]

Where back in those bygone days of yore
The colonel said Ulster must hold out for more
Yet his nine counties into six would not finally go
So they ditched 70,000 brethren and put on a big show.[72]

Near the Broad Road gates of that demesne
A senior garda came with some of his men
To check out the device left in a tea chest
It exploded killing Inspector Sam in the blast.[73]

In Belturbet where Breffni kings once had their home,
We pay homage to two young lives lost in a UVF bomb,[74]
A marina now nestles in the heart of this town
Linking the great waterways of Erne and Shannon.

But north of here, on the road to Enniskillen,
The Bullocks were slain and the cost of the killing[75]
Was total destruction of the old bridge at Aghalane,
Now Mitchell's peace bridge connects them again.[76]

Louis Leonard was killed in his own butcher shop[77]
Then Saunderson, Murphy, and John Maddocks.[78]
Two years of bloodletting in the wee village of Derrylin
Before it spawned the empire of the once Mighty Quinn.

Seán built his huge business from a hole in the ground
Creating thousands of jobs for all the folk round
Then he banked it all on an all-or-nothing wager
Losing the lot though it still bore his nomenclature. [79]

While Quinn was forced to leave the stage
'Dublin Jimmy' stepped in to feed on local outrage
Running his border rackets with no regard to the law
But when Lunney was abducted he went much too far.[80]

And south of the upper lough an ancient frontier
Divides the dioceses of Clogher and Kilmore
The sound of old allegiance is still there by the way
In the accents of Knockninny and Kinawley today.

From the Humours of Ballyconnell we divert once more
To pay our quick visit to the town of Ballinamore
Where famed Shergar's said to have run his final race
In another gambling episode that ended in disgrace.[81]

So from the border districts round Slieve Rusheen
As angels fear to tread where the devil has been,
We take a Stairway to Heaven our souls to save
And find some respite in the Marble Arch caves.[82]

Florence Court nestles nearby in Georgian glory
With National Trust delights to distract from the gory
Details of a catalogue of UDR and police slain
In the Belcoo killings around Lough Macnean.[83]

This was the scene of an early frontier to-do
When the IRA stormed the barracks in 1922
Taking fifteen hostages from the old RIC
They were all RUC by the time they were free.[84]

And near Blacklion the legendary Shannon Pot
Reminds of what we should do and what we cannot[85]
Today that message might just mean rehab
At Loughan House where they held the IRA's 'Slab'.[86]

Back by Derrygonnelly we see Donegal from afar,
Rising up from the Erne beyond Lough Navar
But before we go there we divert back by Melvin
To hunt for Gillaroo in the wee cove of Garrison.[87]

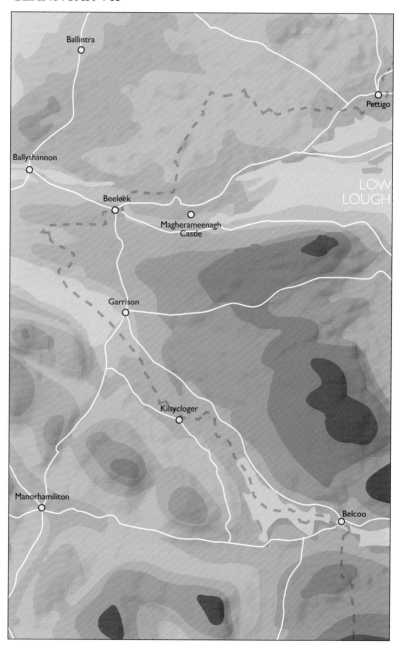

CEANNTAR VII

From rebel Mac Diarmada's stony woods we set out[88]
To view the watery border that lies hereabout
Where the Erne falls into the great wild Atlantic
And an early border invasion caused Unionist panic.

As Collins' plans for the invasion came a cropper
And IRA northern divisions simply had to drop her[89]
Comrades joined up to show the West was awake
As armed men moved into the town of Belleek.[90]

Then gun-toting Hazel was the Orange lady of the lough
Steering a boatload of Specials right up to the dock,
Of the Pettigo triangle occupied by the old IRA
When the Crown brought its big guns to clear them away.[91]

For decades thereafter the Bundoran Express
Shunted Ulster to the seaside to rest and relax
While dipping and dancing and cutting a dash
In breaks for the border that cost all their cash.

We were only teens when the Troubles broke out
Mingling in Bundoran with never a doubt
Things would get better, but how could we know
They'd last all the years as our own kids would grow?

In a grim seaside hotel we gathered to see
The Battle of the Bogside on a black and white TV
And as two armies were sent up to the front
We watched boys our own age still bearing the brunt.[92]

Our anger was growing as they stood idly by
We protested loudly demanding to know why
Then Ballyshannon burst like a dam on the Erne
When they lifted Joe O'Neill from his own tavern.[93]

But bar-stool heroes still sang out summer refrains
About Old Brigade boys and A Nation Once Again
Yet as the years passed those songs lost their lustre
As the Troubles continued to engulf all of Ulster.

Border Protestants around Garrison all moved away
When the UDR's Fletcher was shot by the IRA.[94]
Then Michael Leonard lost the chase on a border track
And as he raced for the line and was shot in the back.[95]

The IRA's Fleming drowned in a Bannagh flood
His comrade Antoine was shot down where he stood
As SAS man Ian Slater was killed in the same ambush
When they thwarted an IRA bomb at Drumrush.[96]

Then the world recoiled in shock and dismay
When a poppy day explosion blasted 12 lives away
So Enniskillen was added to the lists of outrage
While a Tullyhommon bomb just failed to engage.[97]

But IRA misadventures weren't over by far
When Gillian was riddled in her own daddy's car.[98]
In west Fermanagh the botched list only got worse
As Hassard, Love and Keys were added, of course.[99]

Now Orange ranks are depleted in old Donegal
But every July border lodges come one and all
Each with a big banner and its own marching band
To spend a day tramping round Rossnowlagh strand.[100]

I take a rhododendron road through Pettigo
To see an old rebel and socialist before I go
By saintly Lough Derg in the Lettercran earth
Mary rests though questions linger on her death.[101]

We take leave by Scraghey's circles of stone[102]
As we're heading off into the county Tyrone
And as our fickle frontier continues to coil
We leave the Erne watershed for that of Foyle.

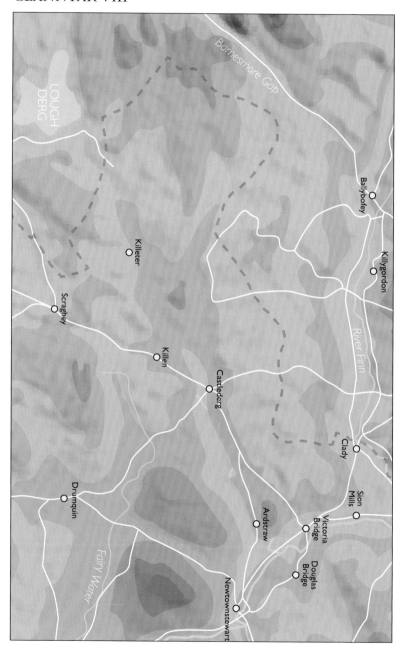

CEANNTAR VIII

Aghyaran balloons out to the Barnsmore Gap
Turning our border world bottom over top
Where the Finn in the South lies just to the north
And the Killen fields flow to the Derg river's mouth.

His youngsters watched him die in an IRA trap,[103]
Within a fortnight she was killed in an evil tit-for-tat;[104]
Two horror deaths at one small village post office
Remembered alone because their dead are not 'of us'.

So Young Loyalists march along the frontier with pride
Recalling bandsmen Michael and Norman who died,[105]
While David's in tears for his lost sister Heather
They were both on patrol and almost taken together.[106]

And when republicans parade to recall their own dead
From Ferguson's Crescent up the Castlefinn Road
To the unattached observer the tunes sound the same
Whether they're playing The Sash or the Patriot Game.[107]

Winston Donnell was the first UDR man to die,
Shot dead on patrol near the bridge at Clady,[108]
Yet young Protestant men continued to join
In the footsteps of fathers who fought at the Boyne.

In a corner of the graveyard on the Drumquin Road
Lie some of those who reaped what division sowed
Armed and uniformed as servants of the Crown,
Many were off duty when they were gunned down.[109]

An evil Omagh bomb was the final full stop[110]
On a sentence of death that formed the backdrop
For separated lives of fear and suspicion
'Til Good Friday's pact came to heal the division.

By a confluence of streams the rivers now pool
Drumragh, Camowen, Fairy Water and Strule,
At Newtown, the Glenelly joins Owenkillew
Meeting the Derg to form the Mourne we knew.

From a checkpoint tower the squaddies looked down
As Mourne now meets Finn at the edge of two towns
Two counties, two rivers now Foyle'd in lock-step
The border lies between them, lest you'd forget.

Back in the day, Donegal's lads and lasses
Flocked to the hiring fair to join the masses
Looking for strong farmers to give them a job
Back-breaking drudgery for just a few bob.[111]

The jobs had all gone when the Troubles broke out,[112]
And the failure of partition never left any doubt
That west of the Bann, the future was bleak
As gerrymandered wards were just given a tweak.[113]

For Donegal's Eddie and English Rose an IRA era began
When they hijacked a chopper and flew over Strabane[114]
With a pass to the cubs at the Head of the Town
They turned for the barracks and rained the bombs down.

The bombs kept coming and every single boom
Sounded another sad chapter in Strabane's doom[115]
As each day began with no work and no hope
 Soon the 'Ra' and the 'IRPs' could barely cope

With queues of young martyrs toeing up to the line
And the youngest of them all was David Devine
Cut to pieces in a hail when the SAS went in,
Along with his big brother and Charlie Breslin.[116]

A huge retail sprawl now fills the space left
When the squaddies flew from their Camel's Hump nest[117]
And with peace again the 'Tinnies' moved in
And invited one and all to 'Let the dance begin'.[118]

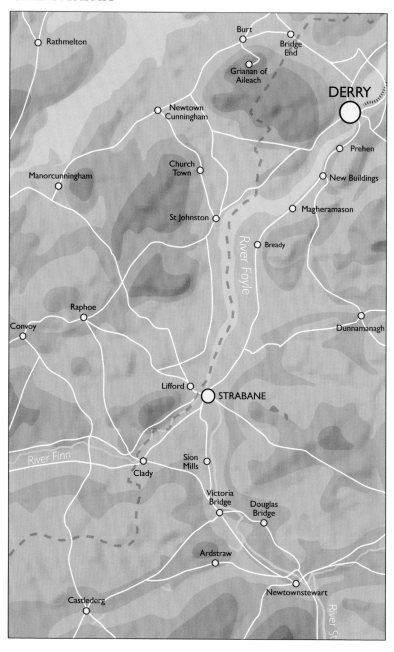

CEANNTAR IX

East Donegal was slated to be switched
In the 1925 report they summarily ditched,[119]
Still Ulster Scots linger in the Laggan's rich soil
As Ballymagorry and Bready peep over the Foyle.

We backtrack the course that Docwra went along
When he took on Tír Eoghan and fortified Dunnalong,[120]
Past St Johnston and Carrigans we now find our way
With Magheramason opposite at the foot of a brae.

Into the city we sweep past a scene of abuse
For foul crimes against weans have no border excuse.[121]
Then into the Bogside and its Free Derry Wall
Where 50 years of domination started to fall.

At the time of partition, Derry city was strong
With shirt factories, the port and whiskey, along
With five railway lines and a big hinterland
But it all fell off the rim of Northern Ireland.

Second city or fourth,[122] it never mattered much
For always when it came right down to the crunch
On jobs, votes or university,[123] there was no chance
When stacked up against the unionist stance.

Yet World War II was a blessing for a city beset
With 20,000 sailors then caught in its net [124]
And the Sixties showed there was no 'us' and 'them'
When crossing the floor to dance up at the 'Mem'.[125]

So McCann, McClenaghan, Cooper and Hume[126]
And all of their comrades could only assume
That protest and publicity would win them the day
But after Bloody Sunday, the IRA held sway.[127]

The Troubles had started and first to die
Was a Derry man called Sammy Devenney [128]
Yet as the death tolls rose, each side could see
Only those who fitted into their own story.

Still for a good while Free Derry held out
Till its barricades fell to the Motorman's clout [129]
Then many others felt the law's full measure
When lifted and held 'at Her Majesty's pleasure'.[130]

Then the sides dug in and the shooting started
While many neighbours and good friends parted
As the city was changed on both sides of the river
Till only the Fountain hung on as a loyalist sliver.[131]

From out of chaos, a young butcher emerged [132]
To lead the IRA as the two sides diverged,
Unleashing a wave of mayhem and murder
That spilled over and back on the nearby border.

And still under siege by their own city walls
Apprentice Boys rallied each year to the calls
To remember the boom and the shutting of gates
They tramped to make sure no one deviates

From grievances and glories over hundreds of years
That spilled onto the streets along with the tears
For Bernadette, Carole, Damien and Annette,[133]
And 13 other children too young to forget.

Atrocities were frequent, but among the very worst
Was one that caused a dam of outrage to burst
When Patsy was forced to drive that deadly device
Right into a border checkpoint and his own suicide.[134]

Then from out of the fire and right into the pan
Stepped Derry's quiet fish-and-chip shop man
With a mountain climber who in turn would meet
The IRA's leader and they talked of peace.[135]

Derry was the very first to give it a chance
As Clinton, Blair and Ahern did their dance[136]
In Guildhall pledges of a fair share from now on
Those vows were broken as soon as they'd gone.

So a millennium and a half since Columba's time
His oak grove still waits for its future to shine[137]
No university, no jobs, and little law and order
It has to make do on its unwanted border.

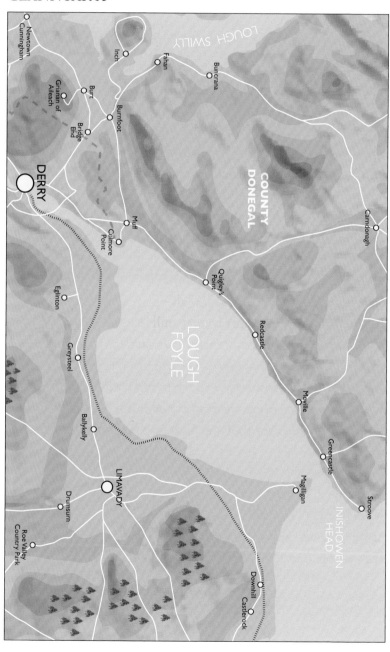

CEANNTAR X

From Aileach's Grianan, Inishowen stretches up[138]
Like a giant speech bubble that rises from Burt
With Burnfoot and Fahan showing the way
To Buncrana's beaches to frolic and play.

And deep in the night the UDA gang
Burst through the door and then bang, bang,
As Eddie lay there in his own pool of blood,
They fled back to Derry as quick as they could.[139]

And from these flowing hills of Donegal
They flocked into Derry one and all
To stitch and sew in a shirt factory mill
So all Derry wans have a Donegal gran still.

But back into the South we make our way forth
Under a bridge of despair we sail to the north[140]
Past Boom Hall, Thornhill and Culmore Bay
With Strathfoyle and Lisahally over the way.

The quays are now silent where the U-boats lay
When Germany surrendered back in the day [141]
As we steer our way out past the last dock
The vast open waters stretch over the lough.

Then from west to east an airplane sweeps
Into the runway that once guarded the deeps
Long after the removal of a double bluff,
When Eglinton replaced the other Muff.[142]

Nobody quite knows where the border sits
Beneath the waves that carry these ships
Around Quigley's Point close by the strand
Where oysters now flourish in no man's land.

Then Eyeless in Gaza the hooded men came
For five techniques without anyone to blame
Among those who locked them in the military lair
Named for an explorer from County Kildare.[143]

And the setting sun over Iskaheen
Lights up the horror from Halloween
When Irwin, Knight and Deeney burst
Into the party to wreak their very worst.[144]

It was another night of horror, truth to tell
When the bombers targeted a Droppin' Well
Eleven soldiers among the seventeen lives lost
The reason given was to teach England the cost.[145]

But back to the lough by a Broighter road
Where a ploughman unearthed his hoard of gold[146]
Left to appease the ancient sea god of yore
As Mananan Mac Lir looks down from Gortmore.

He sees no border on the scene he surveys
From his prow to Moville nestling over the waves
Where liners once tendered passengers ashore
To Monty's dear old Irish home once more.[147]

Bloody Sunday began on Magilligan's strand
Where Paras beat protesters who made a stand[148]
Beside the huts where detainees were caged
As England's killing machine was fully engaged.

Then another Greencastle gazes over the lough
With a Warren Point lighthouse still keeping watch
This time they've shifted to the opposite shore
As if to balance history's mistakes once more.

Then beneath our keel in the Sea of Moyle
A final border passage on the waves of Foyle
We sail out of the border on a Stream of Sorrow[149]
With only the prospects of Brexit tomorrow.

POSTSCRIPT

On our 300-mile canter from lough to lough
We've visited real places and seen the impact
Of localities split and neighbours divided
By a line that none of them ever decided

Should measure where their true allegiance lay,
For none of them was given any real say,
In a quirk of history, a political construct
That started as temporary and then just stuck.

For unlike other borders where people reside
Knowing they differ from those on the other side
On this contested frontier of many deceptions
We identify as Irish with so very few exceptions.

By ties of blood and cultural connections
We've shared our hopes and recollections
Friends and neighbours living side by side
Until politicians imposed a new divide.

So over the course of one hundred years
Measured in days of blood, sweat and tears
We've hoped and coped and counted the cost
Of communities split and so many lives lost.

Families and neighbours caught on the line
Have suffered from partition as if by design
For borders are constructed solely to divide
People from those put on the other side.

ENDNOTES

1 In 1924, Richard Feetham, Joseph Fisher and Eoin MacNeill were appointed as the members of the Boundary Commission established under Article 12 of the Anglo-Irish Treaty 1921 to determine the border between Northern Ireland and the Irish Free State. Parts of their report were leaked in a London newspaper in November 1925, MacNeill resigned, the report was suppressed and an agreement was reached between London, Dublin and Belfast on 12 December 1925 that the temporary border would remain in exchange for the removal of Dublin's share of the imperial War Debt, an estimated £125 million.

2 Carlingford's historical sites include the 12th century King John's Castle and another medieval building licensed as a mint in 1473.

3 Bagenal's Castle was built by Sir Nicholas Bagenal, an English settler from Staffordshire, who was granted the confiscated estates of the Cistercian abbey at Newry, along with land at Greencastle and Carlingford, by King Edward VI in 1552. He was appointed Marshall of the Army in Ireland. His son Henry took a leading part in the military campaigns against Hugh O'Neill, Earl of Tyrone, during the Nine Years War, and was killed when defeated at the Battle of Yellow Ford in 1598.

4 Young Ireland leader John Mitchel (1815-1875) grew up in Newry; Eamon de Valera (1882-1975) was elected as MP for the South Down constituency; Colman Parnell Rowntree (1950-1974) was a leader of the Official IRA when he was shot in a Newry ambush.

5 On 31 July, 1975, Fran O'Toole, Brian McCoy and Tony Geraghty, members of the Miami Showband, were murdered outside Newry in a UVF ambush at a bogus checkpoint as they were driving home across the border. Two of their UVF assailants, Harris Boyle and Wesley Somerville, were also killed in the premature explosion of the bomb they were placing into the band's van.

6 Allegations of a 'Heavy Gang' interrogation team within an Garda Síochána first emerged in the trial of suspects in the Sallins train robbery trial in Dublin in 1978, where claims of physical abuse in custody eventually led to

the acquittal of all the defendants. Amnesty International informed the Irish government that named members of a Heavy Gang interrogation team were also linked to abuse of suspects being questioned in Dundalk and elsewhere.

7 Tom Oliver (43), a dairy farmer and married father of seven from Riverstown, Cooley, Dundalk, was abducted, tortured and shot dead by the IRA on 19 July 1991, on the allegation that he was a paid informer of the Garda Special Branch. A decade later, the exposure of Belfast IRA man Freddie Scappaticci as the British mole codenamed Stakeknife, suggested that he ordered, or actually conducted, the torture and killing of Tom Oliver with the sanction of his British Intelligence handlers, to prevent Scappaticci's own cover being blown.

8 Seamus Ludlow (47), a single forestry worker was found murdered in a lane near his home at Culfore, just north of Dundalk on the Newry Road on 1 May 1976. It is alleged that either British soldiers or a loyalist gang mistook him for a senior IRA figure and a Garda investigation was abruptly curtailed to protect a British mole in the UVF. Contrary to the recommendation of Dublin High Court Judge Henry Barron, no further inquiry has been carried out.

9 RUC Chief Superintendent Harry Breen (51) and Superintendent Bob Buchanan (55) where shot dead when they drove into an IRA trap at Edenappa, just outside the Armagh border village of Jonesborough on 20 March 1989. They were returning home after a meeting in Dundalk with senior Gardai. Their deaths led to allegations of collusion between Gardai in Dundalk and the IRA. A judicial inquiry into the deaths by Dublin Judge Peter Smithwick concluded that while the 'balance of probability' was that somebody in the Garda station passed on information, there was no direct evidence of this.

10 On 27 August 1979, 18 British soldiers from the Parachute Regiment – Donald F. Blair (23), Nicholas Andrews (24), Gary Barnes (18), Raymond Dunn (20), Anthony Wood (19), Michael Woods (18), John Giles (22), Ian Rogers (31), Walter Beard (33), Thomas Vance (23), Robert England (23), Jeffrey Jones (18), Leonard Jones (26), Robert Jones (18), Chris Ireland (25), Peter Fursman (35), Victor MacLeod (24) and David Blair (40) – were

killed and six wounded, when the IRA detonated two bombs in succession at Narrow Water Castle, outside Warrenpoint. Michael Hudson (29), a civilian coachman for Queen Elizabeth II on holidays from London, was then shot by soldiers while birdwatching on the opposite shore across the border in County Louth.

11 On 28 February 1985, nine RUC officers – Alexander Donaldson (41), Geoffrey Campbell (24), John Thomas Dowd (31), Denis Anthony Price (22), Rosemary Elizabeth McGookin (27), Sean Brian McHenry (19), David Peter Topping (22), Paul Hillery McFerran (33) and Ivy Winifred Kelly (29) – were killed and 40 police and civilian employees were injured when the IRA fired nine improvised mortar bombs into their base at Corry Street in Newry. The dead are listed among the 20 officers remembered in the new police station at Ardmore, built on the site of the former Ardmore Hotel.

12 On 1 May 1985, Seamus Ruddy from Newry, a teacher and longstanding left-wing activist, was abducted in Paris by former associates in the Irish National Liberation Army in an attempt to discover details of arms, allegedly obtained from the Palestine Liberation Organisation (PLO). He was listed among the so-called 'Disappeared', those missing and presumed dead. His remains were finally located at Rouen in May 2017 and an inquest established that he had been shot twice in the head.

13 On 27 January 1999, former IRA volunteer Eamonn Collins (44) was beaten and stabbed to death. He had returned home to Newry after being banished by the IRA when he broke during interrogation and gave evidence which he later recanted. He later co-authored, Killing Rage, a biographical account of his IRA activities and gave evidence against Provisional IRA leader Thomas 'Slab' Murphy in a 1998 libel action.

14 The peace and confidence inspired by the Good Friday Agreement coincided with the rise to international fame and success of The Corrs, a family folk band from Dundalk.

15 On 11 November 1957, during the IRA's Border Campaign, Michael Watters, Oliver Craven, Paul Smith, George Keegan and Patrick Parle, were

killed in the premature explosion of a bomb they were preparing within a short distance of the border. They are remembered by the Republican Movement in annual commemoration ceremonies since as the Edentubber Martyrs.

16 Frank Aiken (1898 –1983) from Camlough (Cam Loch) was an Irish revolutionary and politician who served as Tánaiste from 1965–1969, Minister for External Affairs from 1957 to 1969 and 1951 to 1954, Minister for Finance from 1945 to 1948, Minister for the Co-ordination of Defensive Measures from 1939 to 1945, Minister for Defence from 1932 to 1939 and Minister for Lands and Fisheries from June–November 1936. He was commanding officer of the Fourth Northern Division of the old IRA and became IRA Chief of Staff during the Irish Civil War. Originally a member of Sinn Féin, he was later a founding member of Fianna Fáil.

17 On 24 June 1921, on the orders of Frank Aiken, commander of the Fourth Northern Division, the IRA detonated a landmine at Adavoyle, near Meigh, in County Armagh under a military train carrying the 10th Hussars and their horses back to Dublin having formed the guard of honour for King George V's visit to open the new Northern Ireland parliament in Belfast. The blast derailed the train killing three soldiers and 63 horses, as well as the train guard.

18 Harry Thornton from Crossmaglen was shot dead by a British soldier when his van backfired outside Belfast's Springfield Road RUC station on 7 August 1971.

19 Michael McVerry from Cullyhanna, was commander of the IRA's 1st South Armagh battalion. He was the first member of the local IRA to be killed when shot during an attack on Keady RUC station on 15 November 1973.

20 Captain Robert Nairac, military intelligence, was widely known in Crossmaglen as 'Danny Boy' because of the song he performed in local pubs during military raids. An agent provocateur, he also insisted on singing the Republican balled, The Boys of the Old Brigade, in the Three Steps Inn at Dromintee on the night he disappeared (and was presumed shot dead), on 15 May 1977.

21 Captain Robert Nairac has been linked to many murderous atrocities in the area attributed to both loyalist and republican paramilitary groups. They include the Miami Showband massacre on 31 July 1975, the five killed in the 1 September 1975 attack on Tullyvallen Orange Hall, the 19 December 1975 gun and bomb attack in which three were killed at Donnelly's Bar in Silverbridge, along with a simultaneous attack on Kay's Tavern in Dundalk in which two were killed; the 4 January 1976 murders of John and Brian Reavey, and the wounding of their brother Anthony, and the near simultaneous murder of Joseph O'Dowd and his nephews Barry and Declan O'Dowd and the wounding of the boys' father Barney, and the 5 January Kingsmills Massacre in which 11 Protestant workmen were shot with only one survivor, Alan Black. The Tullyvallen and Kingsmill attacks were claimed by an organisation calling itself the South Armagh Republican Action Force, while the Donnelly's bar attack was claimed by the Red Hand Commando, a cover name for the UVF and thought to have been carried out by the Glennane Gang linked to the Mid-Ulster UVF and the murders of the Reavey and O'Dowd family members were attributed to the same Glennane Gang using the cover name the Protestant Action Force. The two UVF members killed in the Miami Showband attack were members of the Glennane Gang and known associates of Captain Nairac. This sequence of attacks was the pretext for the official deployment of the SAS in south Armagh and the ramping up of security operations in that rural district.

22 Leading IRA member Peter Cleary was captured and shot dead by the SAS on 15 April 1976 outside his girlfriend's home at Forkhill.

23 Majella O'Hare, aged 12, was shot dead by British soldier Michael Williams of the 3rd Parachute Regiment, who fired two bullets into her back as she walked to confessions at her local church in Whitecross.

24 British soldier Robert Malcolm Benner from Leicestershire was found dead on a border road outside Crossmaglen on 28 November 1971. He had been abducted by the Official IRA on his way to visit his fiancée in his native Dundalk. James R. Borucki, aged 19, was killed in an IRA booby-trap bomb outside Crossmaglen on 8 August 1976 and commemorated thereafter in the name of the fortified watchtower known as the 'Borucki Sanger' on the village square. They were among 165 Crown forces fatalities in south Armagh during the conflict.

25 Celebrated Gaelic poets Padráig Mac a Liondain (1685-1733), Seamus Mór Mac Murchadha (1720-1750) and Art Mac Cumhaigh (1738-1773) are buried in Creggan churchyard near Crossmaglen. Their legacy is documented by Cardinal Tomás Ó Fiach (1923-1990), President of St Patrick's Pontifical University, Maynooth, who was consecrated as Archbishop of Armagh in 1977 and raised to the College of Cardinals in 1979 as primate of All-Ireland. A native of the Crossmaglen district, he championed academic research on the Gaelic traditions of south Armagh, especially as editor of Seanchas Ard Mhacha, journal of the Archdiocesan historical society.

26 In a 1977 article I wrote for Hibernia National Review, Keeping 'Cross in the News, the widespread disdain of Crossmaglen people for the occupying British forces was summed up in the comment that they 'were not even worth ignoring'.

27 A large part of south Armagh was recommended for transfer to the Free State in the 1925 report of the Irish Boundary Commission.

28 Merlyn Rees was Secretary of State for Northern Ireland (March 1974-September 1976). Among his bungling errors, he lifted the ban on the UVF in April 1974 at the height of its sectarian murder campaign which included the Dublin and Monaghan bombings of May 1974. He designated South Armagh as 'Bandit Country' in the House of Commons, Westminster, on 4 December 1975.

29 Bessbrook Mill, a former linen factory, became the hub of British military operations in south Armagh during the Troubles with troops and supplies dispatched by helicopter to outlying posts and observation towers. In the late 1990s, it was reputed to be the busiest heliport in Europe. The 25 June 2007 formal announcement by the Ministry of Defence of the end of the military Operation Banner in Northern Ireland was illustrated by the last helicopter taking off from Bessbrook Mill.

30 A swathe of mid-Armagh, including Newtownhamilton and Hamiltonsbawn, was settled by Scottish undertaker James Hamilton and his descendants. It is identified as 'scotch country' by many in south Armagh.

31 The County Monaghan district of Mullyash was designated by the 1925 Boundary Commission Report for inclusion in Northern Ireland. The Dorsey in County Armagh was part of an Iron Age rampart in south Ulster that is known at other excavation sites as the Black Pig's Dyke and the Worm's Ditch.

32 On 20 November 1983, three gunmen attacked worshippers at the tiny Mountain Lodge Pentecostal Church outside Darkley village. Three church elders were shot dead at the entrance, Harold Browne (59), Victor Cunningham (39) and David Wilson (44). The gunmen then sprayed the wooden building with automatic gunfire wounding seven more among the congregation of abut 60 people. The operation was claimed by the 'Catholic Reaction Force', thought to be members of the INLA, saying it was 'retaliation for the murderous campaign carried out by the Protestant Action Force', a cover name for UVF in Mid-Ulster linked to the 'Glennane Gang'.

33 In August 1975, Colm McCartney (22) and Sean Farmer (30) were found shot dead shortly after being kidnapped from their car near Newtownhamilton. They were returning home from a Gaelic football match in Dublin when they were stopped at a bogus British Army checkpoint just after crossing the border. The Protestant Action Force, linked to the Glennane Gang and Mid-Ulster UVF, claimed responsibility.

34 The ancient kingdom of Oriel (Airgíalla) was founded in the 4th century and at its peak roughly corresponded to the modern counties of Monaghan and Armagh as well as adjoining parts of Fermanagh, Tyrone and Louth.

35 In May 1595, Hugh O'Neill's forces routed the Crown expedition led by Sir Henry Bagenal in the Battle of Clontibret, the first of several notable Irish victories in his Nine Years War against Elizabeth 1 of England.

36 On 7 August 1986, a large group of loyalists led by Peter Robinson, then deputy leader of the Democratic Unionist Party (DUP), crossed the border at night to protest about lax security on the southern side of the border in the village of Clontibret. They vandalised several buildings and assaulted two Garda officers before being dispersed. Robinson was arrested. In court subsequently, he pleaded guilty and paid a hefty fine rather than risk

conviction which would mean the automatic loss of his East Belfast seat in the Westminster parliament.

37 Dáil Éireann's 'Belfast Boycott' from August 1920 to January 1922 had a huge impact on Monaghan where it was enforced with rigour by the IRA in a town dominated by Protestant businesses served by Belfast suppliers. Retail and wholesale premises were picketed by the IRA, hauled before Sinn Féin courts and fined, trains were hijacked and burnt. The boycott had a devastating impact by severing natural lines of trade and commerce before the border was even set up.

38 The 60-foot obelisk in Church Square, Monaghan, was built to honour Col. Thomas Vesey Dawson of the Coldstream Guards and a local landowning family, killed in 1854 at the Battle of Inkerman during the Crimean War.

39 Just before 7pm on 17 May 1974, a bomb exploded outside a pub beside the Dawson Memorial in Monaghan town. It claimed the lives of Patrick Askin (44), Thomas Campbell (52), Thomas Croarkin (36), Archie Harper (73), Peggy White (43), George Williamson (72) and Jack Travers (28). The explosion was the last of a series of four bombings in Dublin and Monaghan that resulted in a death toll of 30 that day. The mid-Ulster UVF (Glennane Gang) claimed responsibility, though strong suspicion of covert British military assistance through Captain Robert Nairac has persisted.

40 A Monaghan-based 'flying column' of the East Tyrone IRA walked into a trap when they launched an attack on the supposedly vacant police barracks in Loughgall on 8 May 1987. SAS soldiers in hiding opened fire killed all eight IRA men, including Jim Lynagh (31), Padraig McKearney (32), Patrick Kelly (32), Declan Arthurs (21), Seamus Donnelly (19), Michael Gormley (25), Eugene Kelly (25) and Gerard O'Callaghan (29). A passing motorist, Anthony Hughes (36) of Caledon, was also killed and his brother survived being shot 14 times when the SAS fired a hail of 60 bullets at their car.

41 The Hand and Pen Orange hall, built in 1884 at Tyholland, County Monaghan, is now a central exhibit at the Ulster Folk and Transport Museum in Hollywood, County Down, where it was reconstructed in 1995.

42 Eamonn Donnelly (1877-1944) was a politician, party strategist and a passionate anti-partitionist who was born in Middletown, banished from Northern Ireland and elected for Sinn Féin, Fianna Fáil and then Sinn Féin once again to both Dáil Éireann and the Stormont Parliament for constituencies in Armagh, Laois-Offaly and west Belfast.

43 In 1650, James Ussher, Archbishop of Armagh and Primate of all Ireland (1625-1656), published a highly influential 'scientific' chronology beginning with the creation of Adam on 23 October 4004 BC. It proposes that the Second Coming of Christ and Judgement Day would occur around 2000 AD.

44 The 'Battle of the Diamond' on 21 September 1795 was a planned confrontation between rival sectarian organisations, the Protestant Peep o' Day Boys and the Catholic Defenders, which led to the formation of the Orange Order and the 'Armagh outrages' in which an estimated 7,000 Catholics were driven out of County Armagh. Henry Joy McCracken (1767-1798) was a Belfast Presbyterian industrialist and co-founder of the Irish Republican organisation, the Society of United Irishmen.

45 The Glennane Gang, named for a townland in County Armagh, was a secret and informal alliance of loyalists, including the proscribed UVF, the RUC police, Ulster Defence Regiment soldiers and British military intelligence, which murdered an estimated 120 people, mainly Catholic civilians.

46 Dessie O'Hare, aka 'the Border Fox', is a republican from Keady, County Armagh, who has been convicted for torture of kidnap victims and other criminal acts.

47 A convocation in Omagh of nationalist-controlled councils on 19 November 1920 and chaired by Derry City Mayor H.C. O'Doherty, called for an Irish parliament to be based in Armagh City rather than Dublin. This was supported by, among others, the unionist-leaning Portadown Chamber of Commerce.

48 Sir Norman Stronge (86) and his son Sir James (48) were murdered on 21 January 1981 by members of an IRA raiding party who set the historic home alight as they fled across the nearby border. It was burnt to the ground.

49 The 1967 allocation of a newly built house in Caledon to 19-year-old Emily Beattie precipitated the occupation of two houses on the small council estate by Nationalist MP Austin Currie and others. Emily was employed by Armagh solicitor and Unionist politician Brian McRoberts and was engaged to be married to her fiancé from nearby County Monaghan, a member of the exclusively Protestant RUC B Special Reserve. This led to the first civil rights march from Coalisland to Dungannon on 24 August 1968.

50 In the early months of 1922, the Northern Divisions of the IRA were each allocated additional supplies of 500 rifles and up to 300 revolvers for the attack across the border planned by Michael Collins. Many of the guns had been handed over by the departing British army under the agreement that these would be used to equip the new National Army of the Irish Free State.

51 James Craig, 1st Viscount Craigavon (1871-1940) was the first prime minister of Northern Ireland. At the outbreak of the Border War in February 1922, he undertook a three-day tour of the border, travelling an estimated 400 miles in Rolls Royce armoured personnel carriers to reassure the Special Constabulary and local Unionist enclaves that he would back them fully in their armed resistance to any attempt to readjust the boundary.

52 Aidan McAnespie (24) was shot dead on 21 February 1988 by a British soldier after he walked through the vehicle checkpoint in his native Aughnacloy to attend a Gaelic football match.

53 Sean McCaughey died on hunger strike in Portlaoise Prison on 11 May 1946 after five years 'on the blanket' while refusing to wear a prison uniform. Other local IRA deaths include brothers Gerald (29) and Martin (23) Harte, Seán (19) and Pádraig (32) McKearney.

54 Four members of the UDR were killed on 13 July 1983 in a bomb attack on their convoy at the top of Ballymacilroy Hill near Ballygawley on the A5 main road from the Monaghan border to Omagh, Derry and Donegal. The dead were Oswell Neely (20), Thomas Herron (24), Ronald Alexander (19) and John Roxborough (19). Eight British soldiers were killed and 28 others injured on 28 August 1988 when an IRA landmine was detonated under their

military coach at Curr. The attack happened as they were returning to Omagh barracks along the A5. The dead were Jason Burfitt (19), Richard Greener (21), Mark Anthony Norswater (18), Stephen James Wilkinson (18), Jason Spencer Winter (19), Blair Edgar Morris Bishop (19), Alexander Stephen Lewis (18) and Peter Lloyd Bullock (21). The attack prompted British Prime Minister Margaret Thatcher to warn RUC Chief Constable Jack Hermon that she would no longer send British soldiers to Northern Ireland 'in waves to be killed'.

55 Tyrone's Orange County Grand Master Anketell Moutray (72) was among dozens of hostages taken by the IRA across the new border and interned in February 1922. He was reported to have sang out loudly in protest as he was taken away.

56 Columba McVeigh (17), from Donaghmore, County Tyrone, was abducted and murdered by the IRA in 1975 and buried at Bragan, County Monaghan. Despite numerous searches, his remains have not been found.

57 Clogher Valley native Peter Canavan was captain of the Tyrone team in 2003 for the first All-Ireland Gaelic Football Championship victory and was presented with the Sam Maguire Cup.

58 Eighteenth century highwayman Sean Bearna was a local folk hero who raided the lowlands from his base at Strawmacelroy on Slieve Beagh. When border roads in the area were cratered by the British Army during the recent conflict, an annual tradition was begun of organised walks from the three parishes to meet for a picnic and entertainment around the small lake in the Three Counties Hollow where Fermanagh, Monaghan and Tyrone converge.

59 Seamus McElwain from Knockatallan, Scotstown, County Monaghan, joined the South Fermanagh IRA at 16 years of age and was commanding it within three years. Sentenced to 30 years for killing a UDR soldier and an RUC police officer, he led others in the mass escape from the H-Blocks of the Maze Prison on 28 September 1983. He returned to active IRA duty, but on 26 April 1986, he was shot and wounded in an SAS trap near Roslea, along with another IRA volunteer Sean Lynch. His inquest subsequently

found, according to the US State Department and Amnesty International, that McElwain was interrogated by the British soldiers for five minutes before he was shot dead.

60 Volunteers Sean South from Limerick and Fergal O'Hanlon from Monaghan were killed in the IRA raid on Brookborough RUC barracks in the early hours of 1 January 1957. The IRA's Operation Harvest, known as the Border Campaign (1956-1962), was launched from a house in Knockatallan, County Monaghan.

61 After the IRA tried to assassinate Special Constable George Lester as he was opening his Roslea shop on 21 February 1921, his colleagues descended on the village and set fire to Catholic-owned properties, including the parochial house. The only fatality of the night, however, was Special Constable Finnegan who shot himself by accident when using the butt of his gun to break down a door. In a reprisal attack, the IRA raided 16 homes of families linked to the Special Constabulary and shot three dead, including Sergeant Samuel Nixon who had already surrendered and handed over his gun.

62 On 13 June 1643, the Ulster army of the Irish Confederation commanded by Owen Roe O'Neill was ambushed and defeated in the Battle of Clones by Robert Stewart's Laggan army of Protestant settlers from east Donegal.

63 On 11 February 1922, a party of 19 Special Constables arrived in Clones railway station en route from Belfast to Enniskillen. As they boarded the connection train, they were confronted by the local IRA led by Commandant Matt Fitzpatrick, who was shot dead, causing a rapid exchange of gunfire that killed four of the Specials and wounded nine others, along with dozens of civilian injuries. The incident sparked rioting in Belfast and elsewhere that resulted in a further 40 deaths and almost derailed the Anglo-Irish Treaty as both sides retrenched and the withdrawal of Crown forces from the Free State was halted.

64 In 1971, British army engineers began closing most of the 208 cross-border roads. The Clones-Fermanagh interface (about 20 miles) with 49 of these roads, became a focus of the conflict.

65 Wesley Henry Creighton (27) was shot dead by the IRA on 7 August 1972; Robin John Bell (21) was shot dead by the IRA on 22 October 1972; Andy Murray (23) and Michael Naan (31) were stabbed to death by British soldiers at Naan's farm on 23 October 1972.

66 Billy Fox (35), from a generation of Fine Gael politicians once dismissed by their party leader Liam Cosgrave as 'mongrel foxes', was shot and killed by an IRA raiding party when visiting his girlfriend's family home at Tircooney, Clones, on 12 March 1974.

67 The Clones Fáilte Project was set up in 1996 in the former police barracks on the Diamond, to provide support for local Republican ex-prisoners and their families. It was reported at the time that the town had the second highest ratio of former prisoners of the conflict after west Belfast.

68 Barry McGuigan from Clones was crowned world featherweight boxing champion on 8 June 1985. He drew huge cross-community support in an eight-year professional boxing career that started in 1981.

69 The Drummully salient (or polyp), a County Monaghan district west of Clones, is commonly referred to as the 16 'lost townlands' because it is completely surrounded by the Northern Ireland border, apart from a 300 foot (110 metres) unbridged stretch of the Finn River. Directly south of the river, the Monaghan townland of Cornapaste (Cor na Péiste) is contiguous with the Cavan county line near the site of a 1982 archaeological excavation of the rampart fortification of ancient Ulster's border. It is variously known as the Black Pig's Dyke or the Worm's Ditch (Clai na Péiste).

70 At the Battle of Newtownbutler on 31 July 1689, the Enniskillen-based forces supporting William III's claim to the throne won a decisive victory over the Viscount of Mountcashel's forces supporting King James II. The battle ended in a rout with a huge number of Jacobites drowning in the Finn River.

71 On the site of a former castle of the O'Reilly's of Breffni, Castle Saunderson was the ancestral home of the Sanderson/Saunderson family who once had an estate extending for 20 miles on the southern shores of Upper Lough

Erne. It was abandoned when Cavan was included in the Irish Free State at the time of partition by Major Somerset Saunderson who declared, 'Now I have no country.'

72 Colonel Edward Saunderson (1837-1906) of Castle Saunderson was an MP for Cavan and then North Armagh who formed and led the Irish Unionist Alliance until his death, mentored his protégé Sir Edward Carson and signed the manifesto of the Ulster Defence Union to oppose Home Rule in 1893.

73 Inspector Samuel Donegan (63) of Cavan Garda Station was killed in the explosion of an IRA booby-trap bomb at Drumboghanagh, County Fermanagh on 8 June 1972.

74 Geraldine O'Reilly (14) and Patrick Stanley (16) were killed in an explosion in Belturbet when the Fermanagh UVF launched a triple bombing attack with simultaneous blasts in Pettigo and Clones.

75 UDR soldier Thomas Bullock (53) and his wife Emily (50) were killed by the IRA in a gun attack on their home at Killynick, Aghalane, County Fermanagh, on 21 September 1972.

76 A new bridge opened in 1999 was named for U.S. Special Envoy Senator George Mitchell who chaired the Northern Ireland peace talks that led to the 1998 Good Friday Agreement.

77 Louis Leonard (26) an IRA officer in South Fermanagh, was shot dead by loyalists while working late on 16 December 1972.

78 George Walter Saunderson (58), school principal and senior UDR soldier, was shot dead by the IRA on 10 April 1974; James Murphy (42), Sinn Féin member, was shot dead by the UVF on 21 April 1974; John Maddocks (32), a British soldier, was killed instantly when a booby trapped milk churn exploded at Gortmullan, Derrylin, on 2 December 1974.

79 Seán Quinn built a huge business empire, The Quinn Group, from a quarry on his family farm to become the richest man in Ireland in 2008. In

2011, he filed for bankruptcy. The Quinn Industrial Holdings group was rebranded in October 2020 with a name change to Mannok.

80 Career criminal Cyril 'Dublin Jimmy' McGuinness (54) was a leading suspect in the 2019 abduction and torture of Kevin Lunney, a senior executive in the Quinn Industrial Holdings group. He died of a heart attack in England when the house in which he was hiding was raided by armed police.

81 Shergar, a hugely popular five-year-old thoroughbred racehorse, was stolen in February 1983 and a ransom demand was made for £2 million. It is strongly suspected that the operation was carried out by members of an IRA gang who shot the horse within a few days after it had injured itself and that it was then buried on a farm at Aughnasheelin, outside Ballinamore.

82 The Cuilceagh Boardwalk trail, known as the Stairway to Heaven, ascends the blanket mountain bogland of Cuilceagh Mountain that straddles the border of Fermanagh and Cavan between Swanlinbar and Belcoo-Blacklion. Just north of Cuilceagh, the Marble Arch Caves are a tourist attraction protected by UNESCO.

83 On 7 September 1973, UDR soldier Matthew Lilley (54) was shot by the IRA; on 15 May 1976 RUC officers Harry Keys (29), Francis Kettyles (39), and Thomas Evans (33), were killed in an IRA bomb attack; on 25 June 1978, UDR soldier Alan Ferguson (23) was shot dead; on 3 February 1986 UDR soldier John Earley (21), was killed by an IRA remote controlled bomb; and on 15 November 1992, RUC officer Alan Corbett (25), was shot dead by the IRA. The only non-combatant killed in the area during the Troubles was farm worker, Patrick Duffy (21) who accidentally detonated an IRA landmine on 5 September 1973.

84 On 28 March 1922, an IRA column of more than 50 volunteers under the command of Sean MacEoin captured Belcoo Royal Irish Constabulary barracks and took 15 hostages across the new border and imprisoned them at Costume Barracks in Athlone. They were released on 18 July, after the Royal Ulster Constabulary was established on 1 June 1922.

85 Legend has it that the Shannon river is named after Sionnan, daughter of the sea god Manannán Mac Lir, who ate the forbidden fruit of the Tree of Knowledge causing a pool to spring up and drown her.

86 Thomas 'Slab' Murphy was convicted on 17 December 2015 on nine charges of tax evasion by the non-jury Special Criminal Court in Dublin after a trial lasting nine weeks. He served the end of his 18-month sentence at low-security Loughan House Prison near Blacklion. This followed years of unsuccessful investigation into his IRA activities before and after he reportedly became the IRA chief of staff in 1997.

87 The gillaroo, a distinct species of trout, is exclusively found in Lough Melvin which straddles the Fermanagh-Leitrim border.

88 Seán Mac Diarmada (1883-1916), one of the leaders of the 1916 Easter Rising, was born in Kiltyclogher (Coillte Clochair), County Leitrim.

89 Michael Collins established the IRA's Ulster Council in early 1922 uniting all the northern divisions in a plan to annex the Six Counties of Northern Ireland as soon as the British armed forces had withdrawn from the Free State.

90 In May 1922, IRA volunteers from both the pro-Treaty and anti-Treaty factions joined forces to occupy the district bounded by Belleek, County Fermanagh, Pettigo, County Donegal and Lower Lough Erne.

91 On 27 May 1922, Hazel Valerie West (42), ex-wife of Lieut Col Herbert Curling Laverton, steered her steamer pleasure yacht, Lady of the Lake (re-named HMS Pandora) with a large party of Special Constabulary on board up to the dock of Maghermeenagh Castle outside Belleek where they engaged the IRA occupants. While forced to retreat in this battle, the Specials were then backed up by the British military garrison of Enniskillen, including ar-tillery. The Howitzer guns pounded the IRA strongholds and forced them to retreat on 7 June, 1922.

92 The riot confrontation known as the Battle of the Bogside broke out in Derry on 12 August 1969 and lasted for three days, during which Irish army

units were dispatched up to the border and the British army was deployed in Northern Ireland.

93 When Gardaí arrested veteran republican Joe O'Neill at his Bundoran pub in 1970, they took him to Ballyshannon for questioning along with two other suspects. The arrests sparked a lengthy riot.

94 Tommy Fletcher (43), a part-time UDR soldier, was taken from his home near Garrison on 1 March 1972 and shot dead in a hail of bullets.

95 Michael Joseph Leonard (23) from Pettigo was shot by the RUC on 17 May 1973 as he drove for the border after ignoring an order to stop his car because he was disqualified from driving.

96 Antoine Mac Giolla Bhride (27) was killed on 2 December 1984 when the SAS foiled an IRA operation at Drumrush, Kesh, County Fermanagh. His comrade Kieran Fleming (25) drowned in the Bannagh River when attempting to escape. SAS soldier Alistair Slater (28) was shot dead by the IRA in the same incident.

97 An IRA bomb placed near the cenotaph in Enniskillen exploded on Remembrance Sunday, 8 November 1987, killing ten Protestant civilians and a police officer. A twelfth victim of the atrocity spent 13 years in a coma before dying. In the angry aftermath, the IRA called a radio station to report that it had also placed a huge bomb which failed to detonate in the Tullyhommon, County Fermanagh-side of Pettigo where the Remembrance Day parade, including many children, had convened.

98 Gillian Johnston (21) was killed on 18 March 1988 by the IRA which fired 47 bullets into her as she sat in her father's car outside her home near Belleek. The IRA later said the intended target was her brother.

99 William Hassard (59), a builder and his employee, Frederick Love (64), were shot dead by IRA gunmen on the Donegal border near Belleek on 4 August 1988; on 15 January 1989, Harry Keys (23), a former member of the RUC reserve, was shot dead by the IRA outside his girlfriend's house at Ballintra, County Donegal.

100 An annual Orange parade is staged at Rossnowlagh, County Donegal, on the Saturday before the Twelfth of July drawing lodges from the southern border counties and neighbours from Fermanagh.

101 Socialist republican Mary Reid (49) was found dead in mysterious circumstances on a Donegal beach on 29 January 2003. Born in Monaghan, Mary grew up in Pettigo, edited the Irish Republican Socialist Party newspaper, The Starry Plough, was arrested with two others in Paris before being released when police were discovered to have planted the evidence. She was a poet, lecturer and an authority on the Christian sanctuary at Lough Derg. Her family and friends still question the suspicious circumstances of her death.

102 Scraghey Mountain between Ederney, County Fermanagh and Killen, County Tyrone, has a proliferation of megalithic sites including chambered graves, standing stones and three significant stone circles within three miles of each other.

103 William Bogle (27), an off-duty UDR soldier, was shot by the IRA on 5 December 1972 outside Killeter Post Office when he drove up with his three young children.

104 Kathleen Dolan (19) was killed on 14 December 1972 by a suspected UVF bomb as she crossed the street from her family's pub to Killeter Post Office with invitations to her forthcoming wedding.

105 UDR soldiers and members of the Castlederg Young Loyalists Flute Band Norman McKinley (32) and Michael Darcy (28) were killed by the IRA. McKinley died in a bomb ambush on 14 July 1982 while he was on patrol. Darcy was shot dead when he arrived home on the night of 4 June 1988.

106 Heather Kerrigan (20), a 'flag girl' for the Castlederg Young Loyalists FB, was killed by the same IRA bomb as Norman McKinley while on patrol with the UDR on 14 July 1984. Her brother David Kerrigan was leading the patrol and was seriously injured in the blast.

107 A republican parade on 11 August 2013 to honour Gerard McGlynn (18) and Seamus Harvey (22), killed in the premature explosion of the bomb they were thransporting, drew a huge counter-demonstration of loyalists.

108 On 9 August 1971, UDR soldier Winston Donnell (22) was the very first member of the regiment to be killed when caught in a hail of bullets fired by IRA gunmen who pulled up beside his foot patrol at Clady, County Tyrone.

109 Thirty members of the security forces, including UDR and RUC, were killed in the Derg Valley district during the Troubles.

110 The Omagh bombing of 14 August 1998 claimed 31 lives, including near full-term unborn twins and the ages of victims ranged from one-year-old to 65. They included 18 Catholics and 11 Protestants, three from Buncrana, County Donegal, two Spanish visitors, as well as those who identified as republicans, loyalists, nationalists and unionists.

111 Hiring Fairs were held in Strabane twice a year in May and November where boys and girls were hired out for a six months period on 'earnest money' payment of a few shillings to their parent or guardian.

112 Strabane in the 1960s, and for subsequent decades, held the unenviable title of the jobs blackspot of the developed world.

113 Although most areas of Northern Ireland west of the River Bann had Catholic majorities, Protestants controlled local government through extra votes for property owners and gerrymandered electoral wards.

114 Eddie Gallagher from Donegal and former English heiress Rose Dugdale used a hijacked helicopter to drop milk-churn bombs on the RUC barracks in Strabane on 24 January 1974.

115 Strabane and its neighbour Castlederg vied for the title of 'most bombed town' in Northern Ireland during the recent conflict.

116 On 23 February 1985, SAS soldiers ambushed a unit of the IRA returning to an arms dump in Strabane, killing all three. The IRA volunteers were Michael (22) and David (16) Devine and their unit leader, Charles Breslin (21).

117 The huge British Army road checkpoint known as the Camel's Hump commanded the approach to the bridge over the Foyle River between Strabane and Lifford, County Donegal.

118 'Let the Dance Begin', Strabane's iconic millennium sculpture by Maurice Harron of five 18-foot-high semi-abstract figures in stainless steel and bronze, is commonly known as 'The Tinnies'.

119 The Boundary Commission's proposal to transfer majority Protestant parts of east Donegal to Northern Ireland was the breaking point for the Free State government in late 1925. While put forward to balance the transfer of a large swathe of east Fermanagh around Clones, along with south Armagh, to Dublin's jurisdiction, it precipitated the resignation of Eoin MacNeill from the commission and the Irish cabinet. The subsequent deal to retain the provisional border, was a face-saving ploy by Dublin.

120 Henry Docwra (1564-1631) established Crown control of the Foyle in 1600 during the Nine Years War when he led an army into Ulster and fortified Culmore at the river mouth, Derry city and Dunnalong with Dutch-style bastion forts.

121 The official Northern Ireland inquiry into institutional child abuse heard numerous witnesses testify about crimes perpetrated against children in the former St Joseph's Home at Termonbacca overlooking the west bank of the Foyle.

122 Derry is the second biggest city in Northern Ireland and the fourth biggest in Ireland after Dublin, Belfast and Cork.

123 Apart from discrimination in jobs, housing and voting rights, the 1965 decision of the Unionist government to site the new university in Coleraine

rather than Derry, was a catalyst for the creation of the Northern Ireland Civil Rights Association.

124 As the principal naval base covering the vital North Atlantic sea corridor during the Second World War, Derry had huge naval contingents from Britain, Canada, the USA and other Allied countries.

125 Young people mingled quite freely in Derry before the Troubles, especially at dances held in the Catholic St Columb's Hall and the Memorial Hall of the Apprentice Boys of Derry.

126 Eamonn McCann, Dermie McClenaghan, Ivan Cooper and John Hume were among the prominent leaders of the Civil Rights movement in Derry.

127 British soldiers shot 26 unarmed civilians in Derry on Sunday, 30 January 1972. Thirteen were killed outright while another victim died from his wounds four months later. The dead were Jack Duddy (17), Pat Doherty (21), Hugh Gilmore (17), Bernard McGuigan (41), James Wray (22), Michael Kelly (17), William McKinney (27), Gerard McKinney (35), Kevin McElhinney (17), John Young (17), Gerald Damien Donaghy (17), William Nash (19) and Michael McDaid (17). John Johnson (59) was shot twice in the Bloody Sunday massacre and his death on 16 June 1972 was attributed to those wounds in the Saville Report of 2010. The atrocity caused a huge boost in IRA recruitment.

128 Derry father of nine Samuel Devenny (42) was beaten savagely in his home by RUC police officers on 19 April 1969. He died as a result of his injuries on 16 July 1969.

129 On 31 July 1972, the British army launched Operation Motorman to remove barricades from nationalist districts in Derry and elsewhere. It was the biggest military operation since the Suez Canal crisis in 1956.

130 Internment orders issued in the internment swoops of Operation Demetrius in Northern Ireland did not specify a tariff but detained the prisoner for an indefinite term 'at Her Majesty's pleasure'.

131 Through fear and intimidation, an estimated 10,000 Derry Protestants abandoned their Cityside homes in 1969 and moved across the river. Only the tiny loyalist enclave of The Fountain remained below the city walls.

132 Derry IRA leader Martin McGuinness worked as a butcher at the start of the Troubles.

133 Bernadette McCool (9) and her sister Carole (3) were killed in an explosion on 27 July 1970, the first of a total of 17 Derry children to be killed in the Troubles. Damien Harkin (8) was killed on 24 July 1971 when he was run over by an army lorry which mounted the pavement when he was walking home with his friends from a matinée film. Annette McGavigan (14) was shot by a British soldier on 6 September 1971 and is still depicted in a Bogside mural.

134 Patsy Gillespie (42) was forced to drive a 'human bomb' van into a British army border checkpoint at Coshquin on 24 October 1990 while his family were held as hostages by the IRA. He and five British soldiers – Stephen Burrows (30), Stephen Roy Beacham (20), Vincent J. Scott (21), David Andrew Sweeney (19) and Paul Desmond Worral (23) – were killed in the blast.

135 The businessman Brendan Duddy, who started with a fish and chip shop, acted as a go-between from the 1970s to the 1990s for the IRA led by Martin McGuinness and a British military intelligence officer codenamed 'Mountain Climber'.

136 Prime political movers in the peace process that led to the Good Friday Agreement of 1998 were U.S. President Bill Clinton, British Prime Minister Tony Blair and Taoiseach Bertie Ahern.

137 Columba (Colmcille) founded a monastery in an oak grove (doire) in the 6th century (possibly 546 AD) on the site of the current city.

138 The Grianan of Aileach is a circular hilltop fort at Burt, county Donegal, outside Derry city, dating from 1700 BC.

139 Donegal Sinn Féin Councillor Eddie Fullerton (56) was shot dead by loyalists at his Buncrana home on 25 May 1991.

140 Derry has a disproportionately high rate of suicide attributed to social and economic deprivation, poor educational attainment, lack of job prospects, drug and alcohol abuse, as well as the inter-generational impact of conflict. The Foyle Search and Rescue teams frequently focus victim recovery efforts under the Foyle bridge.

141 Nazi Germany's fleet of U-boats surrendered at Derry's Lisahally port in May 1945 and were scuttled and sunk in Operation Deadlight.

142 On 19 August 1858, the village of Muff, county Derry, became Eglinton in honour of the Lord Lieutenant of Ireland, Archibald Mongomerie, 13th Earl of Eglinton who was visiting the locality. It ended confusion with nearby Muff, county Donegal. The City of Derry Airport is located at Eglinton on the site of a former aerodrome used to patrol and provide air support for the North Atlantic sea corridor.

143 During the August 1971 mass arrest and detention without trial of republican suspects by the British army in Operation Demetrius, 14 men were taken to Shackleton Barracks at Ballykelly and subjected to the 'five techniques' of wall standing, hooding, white noise, sleep deprivation and starvation. A 1978 finding by the European Court of Human Rights that this 'inhumane treatment' did not amount to torture has been cited by Britain, the USA, Israel and others to justify gross mistreatment and abuse of internees.

144 On 30 October 1993, three loyalist gunmen of the UDA opened fire on a Halloween party at the Rising Sun Lounge in Greysteel, County Derry, killing eight – Karen Thompson (19), Steven Mullan (20), Moira Duddy (59), Joseph McDermott (60), James Moore (81), John Moyne (50), John Burns (54) and Victor Montgomery (76) – and wounding 19 others. The pub was targeted because it was frequented by Catholics, although two of the fatalities were Protestants. Stephen Irwin, Geoffrey Deeney and Torrens Knight were subsequently convicted of the massacre.

145 The INLA bombed the Droppin' Well disco in Ballykelly on 7 December 1982 killing 17 people, including 11 soldiers. The dead were Ruth Dixon (17), Alan Glen Callaghan (17), Valerie Anne McIntyre (17), Clare Elizabeth Watt (25), Stephen Smith (24), Philip McDonough (26), Stephen Bagshaw (21), Clinton Collins (20), David Murray (18), David Stitt (27), Shaw Williamson (21), Neil Williams (18), Terence Adams (20), Paul Joseph Delaney (18), David Salthouse (23), Angela Maria Hoole (19) and Patricia Cooke (21).

146 The Broighter Hoard of gold treasures dating from the first century BC, was unearthed in February 1896 by ploughmen Tom Nicholl and James Morrow at Broighter on Lough Foyle. The artefacts were thought to have been left there to honour Manannan Mac Lir, the Celtic sea god whose statue now presides over the lough from Gortmore on Binevenagh Mountain.

147 In 1947 when flying over Moville, whence his family originated, Field-Marshal Bernard Law Montgomery of Alamein remarked ,'It looks just the same. My dear old Irish home.'

148 On 26 January 1972, a large demonstration against internment without trial was led along Magilligan strand by John Hume MP. They were confronted by RUC and soldiers from the 1st Battalion Parachute Regiment who immediately opened fire with plastic bullets and batoned, punched and kicked demonstrators. The following Sunday, soldiers from the same battalion opened fire with live rounds at peaceful demonstrators in Derry City.

149 Stroove (An tSrúibh) is the final landfall on Inishowen Head, where Columcille/Columba came ashore at Portkill to gaze back for the final time on his beloved Derry. The placename derives from 'An tSrúibh Bróin' meaning 'Stream of Sorrow'.

MAPS

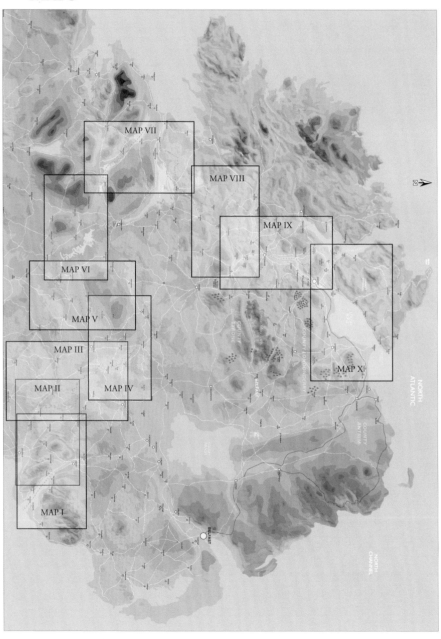